Contracts for Private Investigators

Contracts for Private Investigators

Secrets No One Else Will Tell You

John L. Morris

Author of

Business Basics for Private Investigators
The Evolution of a PI Business

Marketing Basics for Private Investigators
How to Compete as a PI

Sales Basics for Private Investigators
Proven Sales Strategies for PI's

Dedication

I dedicate this book to my grandchildren, whom I will love forever. Kaylee Grace, Harley Mark, Noah Elias, Ezra Jace, Madilyn Shannon, and those yet to join us here on earth however still known by God. Their never-ending energy, innocence, and love inspire me to continue to be better every day.

Introduction

If there were ever a confusing area in the world of professional private investigations, contracts have to be on the top of that long list. Marketing to customers is vital to your business. Marketing is the foundation of your private investigation business's income stream. Without marketing, there would be no opportunity to make sales and get cases that allow you to work and continue your business success.

Beyond marketing, effective sales is also a must-have skill for any private investigator's business. You must know how to close sales when that phone rings. Your marketing gets the phone ringing, and then it is time for you to put on your salesperson's hat. Once you have closed that sale with the customer, what comes next?

After you and your customer have agreed on all of the investigation details and your customer understands the investigation's costs, and after all of the other necessary components have been sorted out, what do you do next? How do you spell out everything you and your customer have agreed upon in a simple and easy-to-understand format while protecting yourself, your client, and all parties involved? Your contract lays out the rules of your relationship with your client and how the work will be executed. These rules are imperative to ensure success in your private investigation business.

Without clearly defined and well-written descriptions for the contract, it is easy for your clients to become at odds with you and your company. Having those explicit and well-written descriptions of each portion of your contractual obligation with your client sets the stage of understanding.

This book will outline why you need to have a contract in place with every client. It will also give you a good understanding of the quality legal language necessities in your investigative services agreement. And last but not least, it will provide you with an outline to write your very own private investigations contract.

Before we go any further, let's look at the definition of a contract. In its most basic form, written or unwritten, a contract must have two elements. These are an offer ("I will sell you this baseball card for $1.") and an acceptance ("Deal!"). Now a contract exists.

There are other elements that come into play. Without getting too technical and legal, let's look at a couple of them. First, the counter-offer ("I won't pay $1, but I will give you $.50 for that card."), At this point, no contract exists. There are three possible paths here – agreement ("OK, $.50 works for me), which creates a contract, disagreement ("No way!), which does not create a contract, and counter-offer ("How about $.75?"), which puts you right back to the beginning, no contract but an offer on the table.

There are other elements like legality (you can't enter into a contract with a minor, for instance), but we won't be going into that level of detail here. Consult with your attorney for more information.

There are many required investments that you must make in your PI business. Investments in equipment, marketing, advertising, networking, and training are vital to success. Your contract, or contracts, should also be a valued asset in your PI business.

Your investment of time, as well as money, in making your contract the best it can be to protect your company will be relevant for years to come. As you go through the exercise of writing your first contract, make sure you take the time necessary to make it right.

Don't just copy all of the text that is in this book. Take time to read each word and examine each clause's legal meaning and definition. Does that definition meet your company's needs? Does that clause make sense for the type of investigative work that you will be conducting?

The cumulative language in these SAMPLE contracts is meant to be all-inclusive, addressing just about every legal situation you may run into out there. However, not every clause, not every section, and not every word may be suitable for your particular situation. Take the time to look over your new contract multiple times and evaluate if it is right for you.

I would also like to encourage you to take a step back and put yourself in your client's shoes. What will go through your client's mind when she reads your contract? Does it seem very one-sided or lopsided from their perspective? Does it only have protections for you and your private investigations business and none for the consumer, your customer?

Ensure your contracts are fair to all parties while still affording your company maximum protection. Make sure your agreements are well written and easily understandable as well. Too much legal mumbo-jumbo can confuse clients. This turn-off for the client can turn into lost sales for your business. I have experienced this myself, back in my early days of being a professional private investigator. When I started, I tried to have my BIG contract for every case, for all jobs, even the simple little things like process serving. The BIG contract was way too much for some of my clients. I often got a lot of flack from many customers about signing a six-page contract for a $75.00 job. Be careful to ensure your contract is not a complete turn-off for your clients. Instead, make sure it is a sign of professionalism in your company.

While I have laid out multiple SAMPLE contracts in this book, you need to keep this in mind. The purpose of these SAMPLE contracts is for illustration purposes only. It is incumbent on your part to seek legal advice before utilizing any of the arrangements outlined in this book or any other contracts you decide to use. Every state has differing requirements for contractual agreements; as well, your PI licensing will have specific required language. You need to know that your contract meets all of your state, county, and local requirements.

Now, let's explore the exciting world of contracts for private investigators as we walk through the process of writing your very own contract, line by line. That is right. You get to write your very own contract for your PI business!

Use the vocabulary and verbage provided in this book, alter it as needed, and make it your very own. Remember, this book and the contents provided are only for illustration purposes. This book's contents should not be considered legal advice, but rather only my personal opinion regarding the subject at hand. I am not an attorney, nor do I play one on television. If you use the sample contracts in this book, you should seek legal advice on the legality and any ramifications of use.

Contents

Chapter 1 - History of my contracts

When I first started as a private investigator, I was overwhelmed with all of the industry's requirements and unknowns. I am sure many of you have felt the same way I did so many years ago. When it came to having a fair contract in place, I was apprehensive about making sure I had the right contract to cover and protect all my needs.

After spending decades working in the corporate environment and having worked with dozens of attorneys over the years regarding literally hundreds of contracts, I built up a reasonably good idea of what a contract required. My experiences include working in retail as well as service industries. I have experience with the business dealings of major corporations, small businesses, publicly traded companies, privately-held corporations, governments, and quasi-government entities.

After all of those years working in upper management for corporate America, working with dozens of attorneys, and reviewing, editing, re-reviewing, and initiating hundreds of contracts, I was able to amass a good deal of sample contracts. I also expanded my knowledge regarding the necessities of an excellent legal agreement between multiple parties.

Those sample contracts I had collected over the years became the foundation for my private investigations contract. I went through the same exercise you are about to embark upon with this book's guidance. The most significant difference between then and now is that I had no book to guide me through the process. I had to roll up my sleeves, grab pen and paper, and start drafting my new PI contract from line one.

The sample contracts we will go over in this book came from those initial private investigator contracts I started way back in 2008. When I made those original contracts, I wanted to make sure I covered all of the bases; as well, I wanted to make sure my clients would be able to understand the agreement quickly, and the contract would have equal protections for them.

After reviewing the complex process, I started on my quest to try to get it right. I decided I wanted to help other investigators through this very process. I could have just gone to an attorney and asked them to write me a contract. I did inquire with several legal experts about the cost of having them write my contract.

I discovered that the cost of having an attorney write my contract would be in the hundreds or even thousands of dollars. Then, an attorney suggested that I write my own contract, and he could review it for me for a fraction of the cost of him writing the contract himself.

This write, review, and re-write process is how I came up with my first contract. That first contract I used is included in this book and is the basis for the exercise you will go through writing your own private investigator's contract.

John L. Morris

Chapter 2 - Do I need a contract?

Let us explore the necessity, or lack thereof, for contracts as a professional private investigator. Most states and many large cities in the United States require private investigators to utilize a contract in some form or fashion. These government entities will often dictate specific content for your agreement and have particular stipulations and terms required. It would be best to inquire with your licensing officials about your local contract and licensing requirements for private investigators.

Beyond government requirements, there usually is no legal necessity for you to use an agreement or contract with your clients. However, even given that there may be no requirement, it makes practical business sense to have a legally binding instrument with all your clients.

The reasons for having a contractual agreement between you and your customer are abundant. Contracts and other legal agreements protect you, your company, your employees, your subcontractors, and your customers alike.

What are contracts?

Contracts go well beyond promises, personal understanding, and verbal agreements in even their simplest form. Verbal contracts often are considered to be legally binding contracts. However, it is often difficult to prove that an oral agreement exists if challenged in a court of law. Courts will often determine that verbal and oral contracts are mostly a "He said, She said" scenario and cannot carry legal weight in a court of law.

Memorializing the agreement in writing can provide much value when two or more individuals, companies, or parties agree to the exchange of services for fees. While many people frown upon contracts and look at them as instruments of complication, they are necessary mechanisms in today's business world. Writing the contract out and having it signed by all parties involved ensures all parties know that the agreement is legally enforceable.

In writing your contract, you should endeavor to be confident that it has enough information to explain the work to be conducted and your client's payment parameters, without being too restrictive and overloaded with detail. Balance is the key. Too many details can restrict, confine, and confuse the agreement's entire scope between you and your client. This book will look at various contracts, from the simple engagement agreement to a fully comprehensive contract.

Reasons to have a contract

Your contract should outline details of the responsibilities agreed upon for all parties involved. A detailed yet easy-to-understand contract allows all parties a reference document to clarify situations when questions arise.

It should also be a binding agreement between all of the parties involved. Binding contracts mean the other parties cannot bow out of the agreement on a whim. Binding contracts should be a benefit for all parties, not just for one.

When another party has failed to meet their obligations, recourse for the remaining parties is another major factor why you need a contract in place. If your client promises payment when the job is done, you need to ensure the client will pay. If your client chooses not to pay, you need the ability to seek legal action and due recourse for their default in the contract.

This recourse works both ways. If you fail to provide the services as described, the agreement allows your client to seek legal avenues of recourse as well. The contract keeps the scales even for all parties involved and should provide comfort to your client, knowing that they have recourse if you do not conduct the work as described.

Your contract with your client also serves as a record of the commitments of work you will provide and help prevent conflicts down the road. This record, and conflict protection, help reduce or mitigate your risk as well as that of your clients.

If you have an investigation firm with multiple employees, that record helps the entire organization maintain compliance with the agreement as written. Maintaining a good description of the agreement is vital for private investigation companies to ensure that each person in the company involved knows what to do and is not working the case or job by memorization, or "how we usually do it."

Contracts also add to your bottom line. Many private investigators never realize this, but the deal does go hand in hand with your sales team. Once you have agreed upon the terms, getting the contract in place and signing it solidifies and finalizes the puzzle's financial piece. You may verbally agree with a client to do a specific job tomorrow for a specified payment without a contract. Once you complete the work, they may say, I didn't know you would do it, you never sent me a contract. Now, you will have little legal recourse to collect what they owe you since nothing was put into writing.

Contracts also emphasize your company's value to your client. You are in the legal profession. Having a contract is a direct reflection of your professionalism. Would an attorney work without a contract? Does any law firm start litigation discussion without a contract? As a professional in the legal industry, you need to have this instrument in place to ensure you protect yourself, your company, and your clients.

Chapter 3 - What makes a good contract?

When considering your contract for your private investigations business, it is good to know what a well-written contract should include. Some of these inclusions may be part of every agreement you have. On occasion, you may have some portions entered into the contract on a case-by-case or client-by-client basis.

Every contract should have a "Scope of Work" section within it. The "Scope of Work" is generally toward the beginning of the contract and spells out, in clear and concise language, what type of work will be conducted.

Scope of work is one of those areas of your contract that will most likely change from one customer to the next. I prefer to have multiple contract templates available for the more common investigative work types I will be conducting. For instance, I have a template for child custody cases and another for injured workers cases, yet a third for TSCM (Technical Surveillance Counter Measures) sweeps.

Having different templates makes it easier for me to get a contract together for a client quickly. Expediting the contract process and getting the client's contract out for signature is an excellent way to close and solidify the agreement.

Time frames are another essential inclusion for a fair contract. Time frames would include defining the period of the initiation of the investigation, when the investigation concludes, and any other pertinent time-sensitive details.

Spell out the money and payments portion clearly in the contract. You need to precisely define how much the work will cost, what billing process is allowable, and when the client must pay. Leaving the financial terms open for interpretation would be a terrible idea and negatively affect your businesses' bottom line.

Discussion on resolving disputes between yourself and your client needs to be in your contract. I have had very few, maybe two or three, occasions where the client and I had a disagreement involving an investigation that we conducted.

Whenever a dispute did arise, I could go back to the contract and help the client understand what we had agreed on.

Now, while none of those experiences ever ended up with the client and me in court or any other legal ramifications, I still had the dispute resolution clearly stated within the contract to ensure we both knew how that would occur.

Things you may consider for dispute resolution is what court venue would any disputes be taken to. In my contracts, this is stated as being in the county where my business is located. This means an out-of-state client cannot simply take me to court in the state where they live, hundreds or thousands of miles away, making it unbearable for me to defend myself.

An arbitration clause may be a consideration you wish to include for dispute resolution. An arbitration clause could state that both parties agree to go to a third-party arbitrator should any disputes arise before filing anything in court. Some contracts will also establish that the decision of the arbitrator is final. As well, this clause might say who would pay for the arbitrator. Perhaps the cost would be 50/50, or maybe it is born by the party who brings up the dispute or paid by the party who loses the arbitration decision.

A renewal clause in contracts is also beneficial for private investigators. I have had renewed contracts on cases multiple times. Having this clause prevents the necessity of having to write the same contract over and over. My preferred method of a renewal clause is merely stating that if the client pays additional retainer fees and we accept those fees, then the contract is extended. The depletion of the retainer fees then terminates the contract. However, the client can continue to provide additional financial resources and continue to extend the contract as required.

It would be best if you also had a termination clause in your contract along with the renewal clause. You will most likely find that typical private investigator licensing requires you to have a reasonable termination clause in your contract.

Warranties and guarantees are something you should discuss in your contracts also. Or, maybe better put, the lack of warranties and guarantees is more appropriate for PIs. I would never guarantee the outcome of an investigation. I will, however, guarantee that I will work to the best of my abilities. "Guaranteeing" your work product is a dangerous and slippery slope, to be sure.

Now that you have a good idea of some of the things your contract, or contracts, need to have, you can start building your own contract. Remember, not all contracts are created equally. In this book, we will cover multiple contract samples. Simple agreements will have far fewer clauses and legalese in them, while more complicated contracts will have everything necessary included.

I prefer to have simple contracts for small, simple, quick-to-perform jobs and more extensive agreements for those more complex situations and in-depth investigations that take more than a day. I will also use my full contract for those situations where I am a little leery about the client or unsure if they fully understand the work's scope. Using the full contract helps protect both the client and me from any misunderstandings down the road.

Chapter 4 - Engagement agreement

Depending on the type of contract you are working with, there will be varying sections and clauses. In this book, we will discuss different types of contracts. This chapter will look at the simplest form of a contract that we will call the "Engagement Agreement."

Beyond a handshake agreement or a handwritten agreement on a napkin, this is about as simple as it gets. Utilize the "Engagement Agreement" for the most straightforward and smallest of jobs that your private investigations business conducts. Engagement Agreements would be used for services such as process serving of legal papers, simple skip trace assignments, or quick spot checks of an address.

In general, the Engagement Agreement would be considered only for assignments for those smaller jobs of a few hundred dollars or less, as well as for projects that will take only a few hours or less to complete. When it comes to larger jobs, it is usually beneficial for all parties involved to have a more in-depth contract.

What should my engagement agreement include?

The first thing your Engagement Agreement should include is a header. Your header for the contract should consist of your company's information and have its name, a mailing address, and phone number.

In our sample Engagement Agreement, we will place the header information into the document's actual header. You can position the header information in the header portion of your document, or if you prefer, you can just put it at the top of the page.

MY PI BUSINESS, LLC

123 MAIN STREET, ANY CITY, ANY STATE, 12345 (333) 444-5555

Sample Header for an Engagement Agreement

The next portion of our Engagement Agreement is what we call the Definition Section. The Definition Section will include the actual name of the agreement. In our sample, this is the Investigative Services Engagement Agreement and will contain the agreement's primary details to have upon initialization of the contract and identifying and defining the parties involved.

This "Agreement" is made this Saturday, January 02, 2025 between John Doe, hereafter known as "CLIENT," and MY PI BUSINESS, LLC, hereafter known as "INVESTIGATIVE CONSULTANT."

Sample Definition Section

Next, our Engagement Agreement will have the Contact Information for all parties. The contact portion should include all parties, their role in the agreement, and any contact information to be used should contacting the party become necessary. This contact information will usually include name, address, city, state, zip, phone, and email.

Contact Information

CLIENT

John Doe

789 Third Street

Doe City, CO 80808

(432) 654-8765

johndoe@johndoe.com

INVESTIGATIVE CONSULTANT

My PI Business, LLC

123 Main Street

Any City, Any State, 12345

(333) 444-5555

joeblow@mypibusinessllc.com

Sample Contact Information

Services to be Provided is our next portion of the Engagement Agreement. Until now, the information within our simple contract has been relatively straightforward. The Services to be Provided section will most likely vary from client to client.

Careful thought should be put into this section to ensure several desired outcomes are met. First, you want this to spell out as simple, yet concisely, as possible the exact work to be conducted. It is best if this is limited to two or three sentences. If the case is more complicated, it may require a more in-depth contract to be in place rather than the Engagement Agreement.

A good rule of thumb is to provide the exact service to be provided, where it will be conducted, if pertinent, and who is involved, such as the subject of the investigation and any other details as agreed upon.

Services to be provided – The parties to this agreement agree that the INVESTIGATIVE CONSULTANT will provide the following services:

Conduct a routine Service of Process of the provided documents from the CLIENT, on Jane Doe, at 3300 Janes Drive, Doe City, CO, 80808. This routine Service of Process will include up to three separate attempts at varying days and times, to be determined by the Investigative Consultant.

Sample Services to be Provided Section

Next on our Engagement Agreement is the Service Payment Section. The Service Payment Section will clearly define how much the client will pay for the services and when payment is required.

It is also good to include in your Engagement Agreement a disclaimer of guaranteed service. This is very easily placed and fits well within the Service Payment section.

Service Payment – The CLIENT agrees to pay the INVESTIGATIVE CONSULTANT for time, material, and services. Payment in full is due upon receipt of the final invoice. A payment in the amount of $75.00 shall be required to initiate the agreement. **The CLIENT agrees that the INVESTIGATIVE CONSULTANT will work to the best of his ability to perform the services within the scope of this agreement; however, the INVESTIGATIVE CONSULTANT makes no guarantees, either implicit or implied, or warranties of service within the scope of this agreement.**

Sample Service Payment Section

You will notice in our Sample Service Payment section, there is a line that states "payment in full is due upon receipt of the final invoice" and a line that states the payment "shall be required to initiate this Agreement." The meaning behind these two lines is to compel the client to pay the invoice once you send it, and this is generally done prior to any work being done.

As well, the second line mentioned states that payment is "required" to initiate the agreement. So, the agreement is not enforceable until it is signed and payment has been made. This protects you from situations where the customer signs the contract and expects work to be conducted immediately, and allows the client to pay at their leisure.

It is always considered best practice to require payment up front from your clients, especially when dealing with clients in the general public, as well as dealing with one-off services or simple services.

Signature lines are required for all contracts, and your Engagement Agreement is no different. This line is placed at the bottom of the document and should include a place for the signature as well as printed name and date for the client and a signature line and date for your business.

_____ Date ____   _____ Date ____

Client Signature   Investigative Consultant

Signature

_____   _____

Printed Name   Printed Name

Sample Signature Line Section

You now have completed your Engagement Agreement for your private investigations business. Appendix A also has a complete copy of the Sample Engagement Agreement, which you did following the step-by-step walk-through.

You need to remember that this is the simplest form of a contract for your business, and should only be used for smaller and simpler assignments and jobs. The more complicated the work assignment, the more protection you will want for yourself, your client, and your company.

Chapter 5 - When and why to use a full contract

In Chapter Four, we discussed and built a simple contract called an Engagement Agreement. While this agreement covers an awful lot, it has minimal protection and provides minimal scope when it comes to the assignment you will be undertaking for your client.

To recap, our Engagement Agreement included the Header, Definition, Contact Information, Services to be Provided, Service Payment, and Signature sections. Our full contract will have all of these sections and many other crucial areas.

You will want to utilize a full contract for most of your investigative work to ensure everything is spelled out, defined, and covered for your protection as well as for your client's security.

Contracts should be a two-way agreement, not just designed to give one party protection and authority. You must also remember, just because it is in the contract, it is not always enforceable. For instance, if your agreement contains requirements of any party that would be considered illegal acts, this would most likely not be enforced or held up in a court of law. If a contract is lopsided or one-sided, then it may be questioned in court also if disputes arise between parties.

You will want to use a full contract for:

- Any case that requires more than a few mundane steps to complete
- Any investigations that have multiple days of work involved
- Any assignment where you will require a retainer
- Any job where you accept credit card payment
- Any job where you may hire subcontractors to conduct the work
- Any case where you will be providing any information to the client
- Any investigation where video or photos will be obtained

- Any assignment involving a restraining or protective order
- Any work that is scheduled out in advance
- Any case where you are not sure an Engagement Agreement is the best choice

The bottom line for the decision process of Engagement Agreement vs. Full Contract, you would be better off to err on the side of caution and utilize the full contract. Your full contract will afford you and your company many more protections over the Engagement Agreement and clearly define many other areas where conflict and disagreement may arise between the client and company.

Chapter 6 - The full contract

As with the Engagement Agreement, you will walk through building your full contract. As we move through this process, we will discuss why these sections are included and why you need them in your full contract. Also, as with the Engagement Agreement, this is only a SAMPLE full contract. You should seek legal counsels' advice regarding implementing your contract and confer with any licensing requirements your state has for you as a PI and for your business to see if additional sections need to be added.

Your full contract will require a header at the top, much like any agreement has. This header should include your company name, address, city, state, zip, and phone number. If you like, you can also include your email address, fax number, website, and other pertinent contact information.

MY PI BUSINESS, LLC

123 MAIN STREET, ANY CITY, ANY STATE, 12345 (333) 444-5555

myname@mypibusiness.com www.mypibusiness.com

Sample Header section

We also need a title for our agreement, a name by which we call the contract. A contract can be called many things like contract, agreement, understanding, arrangement, or several other titles. In general, the word contract is often used, or agreement may be used to soften the name slightly. Either way, it is considered a legally binding, contractual obligation by the court. For our sample, we will use Investigative Services Agreement.

INVESTIGATIVE SERVICES AGREEMENT

Sample Document Title

Next, we have the Contact Information Section. With our more formal full contract, we will take a more formal approach to this section in appearance as well. This section should have full contact information for all parties involved, as well as give a title to each party, such as CLIENT and INVESTIGATIVE CONSULTANT, or whatever title you prefer to call yourself and or your business.

Contact Information

CLIENT

Address _____, **City** _____,

State _____, **Zip** _____

Phone Number _____ **Email Address**

_____

INVESTIGATIVE CONSULTANT

COMPANY NAME

COMPANY ADDRESS

PHONE NUMBER

EMAIL ADDRESS

Sample Contact Information Section

Next, we have our Services to be Provided section. In this section, we first outline that the parties agree that you, the Investigative Consultant, will be providing the services as laid out in this section.

Here, where you lay out the services to be provided, you want to include everything you are providing; however, it is best to put this in as simple terms as possible. For instance, if you are conducting surveillance, it is better to state you are conducting surveillance. There is no need to put mobile surveillance, stationary surveillance, and foot surveillance.

You also do not want to put any language here that may be conceived as a guaranteed work product. An example of what you would not want to put in this section would be "obtain video of the subject." If you cannot "obtain video of the subject," you have effectively breached your contract since you said you would do that.

Even though we have a no-guarantee disclaimer later in our contract, if we say we will do it, then we must do it. Keeping it simple, short, and to the point is always best. If we say we will conduct surveillance and go out and conduct surveillance, and we cannot get a video or get poor quality video, we have still met our contractual obligations.

Services to be Provided – The parties to this agreement agree that the INVESTIGATIVE CONSULTANT will provide the following services:

Sample Services to be provided section

Some examples of how you might use the Services to be Provided section are as follows.

Provide surveillance on Jane Doe, the CLIENT'S wife, to document activities observed. Surveillance will be conducted on Friday, January 1, 2021, Saturday, January 2, 2021, and Sunday, January 3, 2021.

The above example clearly states what service will be provided and what dates it will be provided. Notice, it does not give time frames for the days. You may want to leave the time frames up to the discretion of you, the Investigative Consultant, as the necessary times may change depending on the activity observed.

This example also does not state anything about gaining video or obtaining photos. It merely states "to document activities observed." Obviously, video or photo documentation would be the best, but in the event that no video or photographic evidence is obtained, written documentation may be provided to the client.

Conduct witness interviews, and written reports, of three witnesses, Jane Doe, John Doe, and Bob Doe, at their provided residences.

The example provided here states what you will be doing (interviews) and who you will be interviewing, as well as where the interviews will be conducted. It also specifies that the CLIENT will provide the address for the witness's residences.

Conduct a criminal defense investigation regarding your Client, John Doe, and the alleged crimes committed by Mr. Doe at the Corner Tavern located at 123 Main Street, This Town, CO, 80808. This investigation will include, but not be limited to, review of all provided discovery, prepare and present a criminal defense investigation plan, identify potential witnesses through discovery review and witness interviews, conduct a scene investigation that will identify all video and security cameras at this property, and take photos of the parking area, to include the immediate area where the incident occurred.

The example here is a little more detailed. If your client requests that you do certain specific tasks, it may be good to outline them in the contract. You will notice it says the investigation "will include, but is not limited to…" This language allows you to broaden the scope of the investigation as needed.

We all know once an investigation gets underway, they take on a life of their own. Having specific details outlined that are the only allowed provided services may not be in the best interest of your case or your client, or, in this example, for the defendant.

Keep in mind, though, that there may be times when the scope is narrow and limited by the client. In these events, you should also provide that scope and limitation information in the contract as well.

Conduct a criminal defense investigation regarding your Client, John Doe, and the alleged crimes committed by Mr. Doe at the Corner Tavern located at 123 Main Street, This Town, CO, 80808. Per the CLIENT's request, this investigation will only include reviewing all provided discovery, preparing and presenting a criminal defense investigation plan, and identifying potential witnesses through discovery review.

This language narrows the scope as well as defines why the scope is so narrow. This language is good language to have if the client sees something in your report, then wonders why you did not conduct further investigation.

Other language that should be considered as part of the Services to be Provided section are service disclaimers. These disclaimers include the use of or non-use of illegal or immoral services. A statement from the client states he/she is not misrepresenting anything, the penalties for misrepresentation, and a clear definition of what the client can NOT use any of the investigation findings for.

The INVESTIGATIVE CONSULTANT will NOT knowingly provide illegal or immoral services. CLIENT certifies that he/she is not knowingly requesting immoral or unlawful services and intends to utilize INVESTIGATIVE CONSULTANT services to support legal matters only.

CLIENT attests that he/she has not misrepresented himself, his company, organization, or his/her purpose for ordering searches or requesting investigative services from INVESTIGATIVE CONSULTANT. CLIENT understands that misrepresentation in this agreement shall result in forfeiture of the CLIENT's retainer, and may result in civil and criminal action against the CLIENT and or his/her organization, employees, and affiliates. **CLIENT further agrees that investigative services are NOT for the purpose of entrapment, blackmailing, stalking, or harassment. INVESTIGATIVE CONSULTANT reserves the right to refuse to provide information to the CLIENT for security, safety, unlawful, or immoral reasons, or other reasons as deemed necessary by the INVESTIGATIVE CONSULTANT.**

Sample additional language for Services to be Provided section

---

Believe it or not, there will come a time when a client will want to hire you to conduct an investigation for unscrupulous reasons. Having a clear language that states you will not provide illegal or immoral services, as well as that the client will not request such services, and if the client misrepresents their intentions that they will forfeit their retainer, provides extended protection for yourself and your business.

This type of language also sets the guidelines for which your company operates and holds its employees and subcontractors. In essence, it is setting policy for your company when it comes to illegal and immoral activity.

After we have clarified what investigative services shall be provided, we need to explain how much the client will pay you for services to be rendered. This is done with the Retainer section of our contract.

Retainer – CLIENT shall place $X,XXX.XX in possession of the INVESTIGATIVE CONSULTANT to serve as the initial retainer for services provided by the INVESTIGATIVE CONSULTANT. Should the provided retainer be insufficient to cover all costs of the services provided, the CLIENT shall pay the INVESTIGATIVE CONSULTANT all additional amounts due upon receipt of invoice. CLIENT understands that any unpaid balances, after 30 days, shall incur interest accumulated at 1.5% monthly. **Retainer must be paid in full prior to scheduling or conducting any services.**

Sample Retainer Section

Our Retainer section clearly states how much of a retainer is to be paid to the investigative consultant. This section further explains the client's responsibility to quickly pay all unpaid balances and lays out the interest penalty for any unpaid balances. The last line is of the utmost importance and is another policy setting statement for your company. The retainer "must" be paid in full prior to scheduling or conducting any work. Thus, regardless of when the contract was signed, if the retainer is not paid, you are not obligated to start any work on the assignment for the client.

After the discussion of the retainer comes the discussion of how we bill for our work. If you sell by the retainer many times, this will be the first time your client sees your hourly rate. It is best to have your rates clearly defined and list what is to be charged for outlined in as much detail as possible. This also sets yet another policy for your company to help with maintaining policy standards.

Rates – Hourly rates for Investigative Services, to include all travel time, report time, video and photo editing time, client consultation time, and case management time utilized on the investigation, shall be billed at $XX.XX per hour per investigator in fifteen-minute increments. Further expenses as determined necessary for the successful completion of the services to be provided by the INVESTIGATIVE CONSULTANT will be reimbursed 100%, and all mileage traveled will be billed at $0.XX per mile.

Sample Rates section

With the ever-growing use of online credit cards processing and other electronic payment methods, we must have certain financial protections in place as professional private investigators. While it is not commonplace, from time to time, we may run into clients who have "buyer's remorse" when the result of the investigation is not what they had hoped for or anticipated. As well, there are unscrupulous individuals who may wish to try to take advantage of the situation and then use chargebacks to either blackmail or defraud your business.

This simple chargeback section explains what all charges are for. These charges are for time and expenses, retainers, and other billings as outlined in the agreement. It also provides authorization for the payment to you by the client on whichever account they pay from. Further, it clearly states that the client will not attempt to conduct chargebacks or cancel any payments made.

If you utilize another electronic payment method regularly, you may wish to include that in the list of popular payment types.

Credit Card Authorization / Chargeback or Payment Cancelation – CLIENT authorizes INVESTIGATIVE CONSULTANT to charge the CLIENT's credit card account, checking account, or other electronic payment account, provided to or used to pay, the INVESTIGATIVE CONSULTANT. The amounts charged by the INVESTIGATIVE CONSULTANT are for time, expenses, retainer, and billing as outlined in this agreement. CLIENT waives the right to chargeback or cancel any credit card, electronic payments (such as, but not limited to, PayPal, Venmo, etc.) or e-check, or written check payment.

Sample Credit Card Authorization / Chargeback or Payment Cancellation Section

If there are regular services that you always provide in almost every investigation, you may want to consider adding them to the inclusions list. For your protection, though, the line that states "Further expenses, as determined necessary for the successful completion of the services" should be sufficient to cover for those unknown expenses like running plates, pulling a criminal record, conducting a locate report, etc.

Next, we need to look at a Client Interference clause. Yes, unfortunately, this is a necessary addition for most contracts these days. The provided clause covers both client interference and misrepresentation. The clause is concise and to the point. If you cancel the agreement for client interference or misrepresentation by the client, he/she forfeits their entire retainer.

CLIENT Interference / Misrepresentation – INVESTIGATIVE CONSULTANT reserves the right to terminate this agreement at any time if there is CLIENT interference or misrepresentation by CLIENT or second or third parties directed by CLIENT. Should this agreement be terminated due to CLIENT interference and or misrepresentation, the CLIENT will forfeit the entire retainer for the agreement.

Sample Client Interference / Misrepresentation section

A lot of language in this sample contract holds the retainer as the penalty price for infractions of the agreement by the client. This demonstrates why it is so essential to work on a retainer only basis with most clients.

You can change the language to read something to the effect of the client owing a certain amount that was determined as the anticipated total price of the investigation. However, there are considerable pitfalls to that approach. If you do not have the retainer in hand, you find yourself in the collection business for services not rendered, and you will find yourself more often having to take the client to court for settlement and judgment. If you are successful, you still only have a decision and must still collect the judgment.

Moving along, we have the Accuracy of Information section. This section provides yet more protection for you and your company with two distinct portions of liability.

First, the client is responsible for providing you with true and accurate information. If the client provides you with a wrong address to conduct surveillance on his ex-wife, that will ultimately negatively impact your surveillance's success. This section protects you from being punished for the lack of correct information by the client.

Further, this section lays out some fundamental guidelines for the accuracy of data you provide to your client. If you obtain information from public or private systems, and that information is not accurate, you cannot be held liable. This informs the client they should work to ensure the information is accurate.

Suppose you conduct a POE (Place of Employment) investigation on your client's deadbeat ex-husband, and the data retrieved from your databases proves to be inaccurate. In that case, you cannot be held liable.

Now, this protection only goes as far as is logically acceptable. If you are offering guaranteed services or guaranteed data to be provided, this has little bearing on those services.

Accuracy of Information – The accuracy of information submitted by the CLIENT will directly determine the success of the provided investigative services. INVESTIGATIVE CONSULTANT cannot be held liable for inaccuracies in public record information, databases accessed, or requests submitted by the CLIENT. While the information furnished by the INVESTIGATIVE CONSULTANT is from reliable sources, its accuracy is not guaranteed. All information provided by the INVESTIGATIVE CONSULTANT should be verified as to accuracy, timeliness, and legal applications prior to preparation of reports or usage of information. Information provided may have items that are incomplete, incorrect, omitted, misspelled, or deleted. The accuracy of information provided is not in the control of the INVESTIGATIVE CONSULTANT. INVESTIGATIVE CONSULTANT shall attempt to maintain the integrity of all information and data provided. Information and data collected during this investigation shall be released to the CLIENT or other party intended as per the request of the CLIENT, at the sole discretion of the INVESTIGATIVE CONSULTANT.

Sample Accuracy of Information section

No Warranties or Guarantees is the next big section of our full contract. This essentially informs the client that, while we will work to the best of our ability, we cannot guarantee our investigation's outcome.

So, if you are working on a cheating spouse case, you are not guaranteeing that you will get a video of your client's spouse. If you are working on a criminal defense case, you will not guarantee that you will find the evidence that will guarantee a walk for your client. If you are working on a slip and fall insurance claim, you will not guarantee you will ever set eyes on the subject.

It is never good practice to guarantee anything in this ever-evolving and changing profession of private investigation. The best guaranty you can provide is to work to the best of your abilities.

No Warranties or Guarantee – Neither the INVESTIGATIVE CONSULTANT nor its employees or agents have made any warranties nor guarantees as to the success or outcome of the investigation, research, or matters involved in the investigative services to be provided for the CLIENT. CLIENT understands that investigations are, by their nature, limited by time and resources and may not produce the final product that the CLIENT had desired or intended.

Sample No Warranties or Guarantees Section

An indemnification clause is an absolutely essential part of your full contract. This portion of your contract lays out the responsibility of defending you against third-party actions in the event the client provides inaccurate or misleading information regarding the investigation.

In other words, if the client provides you with detailed information that makes you go a specific direction in your investigation, and that direction you chose inadvertently violates another person's rights, the client is responsible for the costs involved in protecting you regarding that matter.

However, what the indemnification clause does not do is protect you if you are acting on the information you acquire during the investigation, or willfully, inadvertently, or negligently do something illegal or immoral during the investigation.

Finally, the last line of the indemnification clause protects you against liability for anything you may do in the investigation that provides liability to the client in legal, financial, or even incidental damages.

Now, you should take that with a grain of salt too. If you intentionally, willfully, or negligently open your client up to liability, you can be held liable by your client regardless of what clauses you have in your contract.

Indemnification of INVESTIGATIVE CONSULTANT from CLIENT Provided Information – The CLIENT agrees to indemnify and hold the INVESTIGATIVE CONSULTANT, its employees, and agents harmless against all claims, damages, losses, expenses, liabilities and / or CLIENT or third-party actions arising out of or related to any information which the CLIENT provided to the INVESTIGATIVE CONSULTANT prior to or during the conduct of services provided. INVESTIGATIVE CONSULTANT, its employees, and agents shall not be liable for any legal, financial, incidental, or consequential damages of any type.

Sample Indemnification Section

The refund section is not necessary but can be extremely helpful for you in your contract. Thus far, I have had only a single request for a refund from a client throughout my career. This low number is astounding, considering that I have had thousands of contracts over the years.

This low, almost non-existent number of refund requests can be directly attributed to the language in my contract that states we cannot guarantee results in this non-refund clause.

One thing to keep in mind is that this is a non-refund clause due to the results not being what the client anticipated or desired. If there are unused retainer funds, though, no matter the reason, you are obligated to refund those unused fees.

Refunds – Based on the nature of investigative work, we are unable to guarantee the desired result of the CLIENT. Therefore, we do not issue refunds for our services rendered. In the event there are unused retainer funds after all investigative services have been completed, the INVESTIGATIVE CONSULTANT shall refund all unused retainer funds within thirty days of completion of the investigation.

Sample Refunds Section

All good things must come to an end, and that goes for contracts with your clients as well. Regarding your contract, you want to have a well-thought-out termination for the agreement that allows for several considerations.

This termination clause states that once all of the work is done, or you run out of retainer funds, the contract is terminated. However, suppose there is more work to be conducted, and you and your client agree to continue the investigation. In that case, the agreement is extended with the same terms upon you accepting and receiving more retainer funds.

Another important piece is an out for all parties in the contract. Most private investigations licenses require that your agreement has a termination clause with specific language. You will want to ensure that this section meets those requirements.

The language allowing early termination by the client in this contract allows them to terminate the contract, with written notice, up to 48 hours prior to work being conducted. It also stipulates that any scheduled work is still billable at 50%, considered industry standard. If you have planned work for two days from now, and your client cancels on you, it won't be easy to replace that work, and you most likely have already turned down or rescheduled other potential assignments for those hours.

Termination of Agreement – This Agreement shall remain in effect until all retainer funds have been exhausted. or until all services are completed as agreed. This agreement may be terminated by either party with 48 hours written notification. If CLIENT terminates this agreement early for any reason, all scheduled work shall be billed at 50% (fifty percent). This agreement can be extended upon the acceptance and receipt of additional retainer funds at the discretion of the INVESTIGATIVE CONSULTANT.

Sample Termination Section

Restraining orders and protective orders are serious business and should be handled with extreme care in the private investigations field. Many times, bad guys, looking to harm, will try to hire the unsuspecting PI to find someone under false pretense. This is often done under the guise of attempting to find an old high school buddy, brother, or sister estranged by the family. These are great reasons for you, as the professional in the relationship, to conduct your due diligence and check every client's story to ensure that they have the legal right to pursue the action requested.

Restraining / Protective Orders – Investigative Consultant will not conduct any investigative services or obtain any information for a CLIENT who has a restraining or protection order placed on them. In the event such an order is in place, and the CLIENT has not disclosed this information to the INVESTIGATIVE CONSULTANT, this agreement will be terminated upon discovery of this information by the INVESTIGATIVE CONSULTANT, and the full retainer shall be forfeit by the CLIENT.

Sample Restraining / Protective Order Section

Another common practice within the private investigation profession is the use of subcontractors for specific projects and assignments. You may need to utilize a subcontractor when you are too busy to handle all the workload yourself. Or you may also need to utilize subcontractors with specific and unique qualifications and skills for more extensive cases. And sometimes, you need to use multiple investigators due to the complexity of a case, such as multi-day, 24-hour surveillance.

In this subcontractor section of our contract, we are notifying the client that we may use subcontractors on an as-needed basis; as well, it is at our discretion whether we do so or not.

Use of subcontractors – It is the discretion of the INVESTIGATIVE CONSULTANT to use subcontractors on an as-needed basis. INVESTIGATIVE CONSULTANT will only use qualified subcontractors with the proper licensing, insurance, and skills required. Due to assignment complexities, it may be necessary for the INVESTIGATIVE CONSULTANT to use multiple investigators throughout the assignment. Use of multiple investigators is at the discretion of the INVESTIGATIVE CONSULTANT.

Sample Use of Subcontractors Section

Confidentiality is an absolute necessity for legal agreements and relationships. Not only is it a necessary part of the relationship between client and private investigator, but it is also required under most private investigator licensing laws and rules. This is another area where you can use your contract language to spell out your company's policy on confidentiality for all to know and understand.

Confidentiality – CLIENT understands that all provided findings, reports, videos, photos, data, and other investigative information from the INVESTIGATIVE CONSULTANT are exclusively for the use of the CLIENT. CLIENT agrees to limit access to these findings, reports, videos, photos, data, and other information to third parties who have a legitimate legal need to know and / or are authorized by law. CLIENT holds INVESTIGATIVE CONSULTANT, its employees, subcontractors, managers, owners, and other associates harmless from damages, losses, costs, and expenses, including attorney fees suffered or incurred due to claims based on investigative findings provided to the CLIENT. INVESTIGATIVE CONSULTANT will keep all investigative findings confidential and will not disseminate any findings to third parties unless authorized in writing by the CLIENT or ordered by a court of law in the United States of America.

Sample Confidentiality Section

Your contract should most definitely include this next section, which outlines what jurisdiction is acceptable for legal proceedings. In the unfortunate event that you and your client have a misunderstanding, and either need to take the other party to court, this outlines what jurisdiction this would be done in.

Typically, you would want to put in the county and the state where you reside or where your business office is located. Therefore, if your customer is a thousand miles away, in another county and state, he must file any claims against you in a court where you reside.

The reasons for wanting to make sure any legal actions are in your county and state are numerous. First, it makes it much easier for you, as the venue is close to you. Secondly, if you have to file a claim against your client, you can do so with a court close to you for collection on debt or breach of contract. You most likely will have more knowledge about a nearer court, too. And, if you have an attorney representing you, that attorney is not racking up high travel expenses to defend or represent you and your company.

Jurisdiction for Legal Proceedings – Any legal proceedings initiated by the CLIENT toward INVESTIGATIVE CONSULTANT shall be within Your County, Your State.

Sample Jurisdiction for Legal Proceedings Section

The signature block is the final piece of the puzzle for your full private investigations contract. This is also one of the most critical components of the entire agreement. This is where you and your Client sign, date, and write your printed name. This signing process then legally memorializes the contract.

There is also a disclaimer line at the top for electronic signature means. Given the ever-expanding world of electronic documentation, this is vital to make sure it is included. If you use any particular online service for completing e-signatures, you may want to add that to the list as well; however, it should be covered with the generic language we have.

If you find yourself in a situation where there are multiple signers to the agreement, let's say you are contracting with a partnership and they want all partners to sign off on it, then you can add additional client signature lines as needed. If you need to do this, you may want to make the first signature line read as CLIENT Signature (Primary CLIENT contact). This will help ensure you only have to work directly with one individual or client.

The validity of signatures on faxed, emailed, or other electronically disbursed versions of this contract shall be the same as the original.

_____ Date _____

CLIENT Signature

_____

CLIENT Name (Spelled)

_____ Date _____

INVESTIGATIVE CONSULTANT Signature

_____

INVESTIGATIVE CONSULTANT Name (Spelled)

Sample Signature Block

That is the conclusion of the complete contract for your PI business. Feel free to adjust, edit, and write it to fit your business needs best. Next, we will look at other less common types of legal agreements and contracts.

Chapter 7 - **Email, verbal and other contracts**

At this point, you should have a relatively good understanding of what your contract should include and the language necessary to protect all parties involved. But what about those special occasions where a formal agreement is never entered into? How do you handle those?

It is common in this day and age for legal contracts to be laid out and solidified via email. One thing you should always keep in mind, in most legal jurisdictions in the United States, any agreement between two parties can be considered as a binding contract. So, if your client emails you a job assignment, and you accept that assignment, then, in effect, you have a contract with your client.

As an example, if your client is an attorney, and he sends you an email with case information, a list of investigative work for you to perform, and you reply with a simple, okay, then you have essentially entered into a legal agreement for that work.

To further protect yourself and your company, I suggest replying with something a little more definitive. An acceptable reply may look like this. "Thank you; we will get started on this assignment as soon as our schedule allows. I would anticipate concluding this investigation within three weeks and with an estimated budget of $1,500.00 - $2,000.00."

Now you have set additional parameters to the agreement. You have just laid out the foundation for a time frame within which you will conduct the work, a cost for the work, and accepted the job as assigned initially. Concise communication with your client will ensure you both have a good understanding of what to expect.

Is this type of communication necessary for your relationship with your client? The answer to that question will depend on how the working partnership has gone up to this point. However, I always use caution, even with long-term clients, to ensure my legal side is covered.

You never know when a business relationship will end for any reason. Always think through your email responses to your clients. And always remember, everything you say in an email can be construed as a legally binding agreement.

Verbal or handshake agreements

Regardless of how the agreement is formulated, all arrangements may be considered to be legally binding contracts. You may have heard of "handshake" agreements. Handshake agreements, also known as "verbal agreements," are more common than many people think and can lead to a lot of headaches if not thought out properly.

If you ever find yourself in the middle of a situation where you may be entering into a legally binding agreement with a client via verbal means, you should consider the following things.

You can always bow out gracefully just by saying something to the effect of, "That is a good start. I can go back to the office and draft a short letter of agreement for us and email it to you today." Stating your position in this way essentially tells the client you are not entering into a verbal agreement. Instead, you will complete a written contract for them to consider.

Another consideration when you are about to enter into a verbal agreement is to solidify it via email. After you have agreed upon the terms, you send an email to the client, laying out what was discussed. Once the client has responded and accepted the terms as laid out in that email, you have a written agreement. Text is another way to memorialize the deal too, but if possible, email would be my preferred method.

As stated previously, a handshake agreement is a viable and legally binding agreement. It is much harder to prove in a court of law, especially if you and your client are the only two witnesses. With that said, I would recommend having someone present with you if you think you may ever get into a situation where you would be entering into a handshake agreement.

A handshake agreement does not necessarily require a physical handshake either. Simple comments like "Let's do it" or

"Sounds good" are just as much a signature or handshake and just as binding.

Myself, I never make this type of agreement with clients. I always make sure I end those conversations with a statement that I will get everything outlined in a formal agreement and send it to the client. This ensures that the client knows we do not yet have a legal arrangement, but one is forthcoming.

Invoice contracts

I use what I refer to as an invoice contract for the very simplest of jobs with my businesses. Process serving is a great example. For a routine serve, my invoices contain the following language.

"STANDARD SERVE - FIRST ATTEMPT IN FOUR BUSINESS DAYS AFTER RECEIPT OF DOCUMENTS AND PAYMENT, UP TO THREE TOTAL ATTEMPTS."

As well, my invoice states that invoices are due upon receipt. This, in effect, makes my invoice a legally binding agreement. It states what work is to be conducted (standard serve), states when it will be conducted (after receipt of documents and payment), and of course, the cost is in the invoice.

Once the client has made the payment, they have effectively accepted the terms of the agreement. This is an easy and effective way to enter into an agreement with your client and send an invoice for payment without having an over burdensome contract.

When I first got into the process serve business, I required an actual contract. This initial contract was very similar to the Engagement Agreement as laid out earlier in this book. I quickly discovered, though, that most clients felt this was an unnecessary step in the process.

I also discovered that creating a contract for these smaller jobs affected my bottom line and per-hour income for the business. I was spending more time on many serves, putting a contract together and ensuring the client signed it than I was conducting the actual service and producing an affidavit.

Conclusion

The more complex the deal is, the more work involved, and the larger the investigation will be, the more sophisticated your contract should be. If I have to leave you with any single piece of information, you are always better to err on the side of caution and use a more extensive contract when in doubt.

You can adjust your policies regarding contracts to grow your business and further understand what your clients need. However, you cannot make a customer enter into a more complex agreement once they have agreed to what you had first presented.

As outlined in the last section of this book, there are many creative and simple contracts for those smaller jobs. I always recommend getting the final agreement in writing, whether it is a full-blown contract, a simple engagement agreement, email, text, or invoice.

Covering your legal "Six" is vital in this business. Contracts can do just that, as well as protect your client equally. In the legal industry we work in, having a good contract for every case is considered one of the highest professional levels.

Appendix A – Sample Engagement Agreement

MY PI BUSINESS, LLC

123 MAIN ST, ANY CITY, ANY STATE, 12345 (333) 444-5555

This "Agreement" is made this Saturday, January 02, 2025 between John Doe, hereafter known as "CLIENT," and MY PI BUSINESS, LLC, hereafter known as "INVESTIGATIVE CONSULTANT."

Contact Information

CLIENT

John Doe

789 Third Street

Doe City, CO 80808

(432) 654-8765

johndoe@johndoe.com

INVESTIGATIVE CONSULTANT

My PI Business, LLC

123 Main Street

Any City, Any State, 12345

(333) 444-5555

joeblow@mypibusinessllc.com

Services to be provided – The parties to this agreement agree that the INVESTIGATIVE CONSULTANT will provide the following services:

Conduct a routine Service of Process of the provided documents from the CLIENT, on Jane Doe, at 3300 Janes Drive, Doe City, CO, 80808. This routine Service of Process will include up to three separate attempts at varying days and times, to be determined by the Investigative Consultant.

Service Payment – The CLIENT agrees to pay the INVESTIGATIVE CONSULTANT for time, material, and services. Payment in full is due upon receipt of the final invoice. A payment in the amount of $75.00 shall be required to initiate the agreement. **The CLIENT agrees that the INVESTIGATIVE CONSULTANT will work to the best of his ability to perform the services within the scope of this agreement; however, the INVESTIGATIVE CONSULTANT makes no guarantees, either implicit or implied, or warranties of service within the scope of this agreement.**

_____ Date _____

Client Signature

_____ Date _____

Inv Consultant Signature

_____

Printed Name

_____

Printed Name

John L. Morris

Appendix B Sample Full Contract

MY PI BUSINESS, LLC

123 MAIN ST, ANY CITY, ANY STATE, 12345 (333) 444-5555

myname@mypibusiness.com www.mypibusiness.com

INVESTIGATIVE SERVICES AGREEMENT

Contact Information

CLIENT

Address _____**, City** _____**,**

State _____**, Zip** _____

Phone Number _____ **Email Address**

_____

INVESTIGATIVE CONSULTANT

COMPANY NAME

COMPANY ADDRESS

PHONE NUMBER

EMAIL ADDRESS

Services to be Provided – The parties to this agreement agree that the INVESTIGATIVE CONSULTANT will provide the following services:

The INVESTIGATIVE CONSULTANT will NOT knowingly provide illegal or immoral services. CLIENT certifies that he/she is not knowingly requesting immoral or unlawful services and intends to utilize INVESTIGATIVE CONSULTANT services to support legal matters only.

CLIENT attests that he/she has not misrepresented himself, his company, organization, or his/her purpose for ordering searches or requesting investigative services from INVESTIGATIVE CONSULTANT. CLIENT understands that misrepresentation in this agreement shall result in forfeiture of the CLIENT's retainer, and may result in civil and criminal action against the CLIENT and or his/her organization, employees, and affiliates. **CLIENT further agrees that investigative services are NOT for the purpose of entrapment, blackmailing, stalking, or harassment. INVESTIGATIVE CONSULTANT reserves the right to refuse to provide information to the CLIENT for security, safety, unlawful, or immoral reasons, or other reasons as deemed necessary by the INVESTIGATIVE CONSULTANT.**

Retainer – CLIENT shall place $X,XXX.XX in possession of the INVESTIGATIVE CONSULTANT to serve as the initial retainer for services provided by the INVESTIGATIVE CONSULTANT. Should the provided retainer be insufficient to cover all costs of the services provided, the CLIENT shall pay the INVESTIGATIVE CONSULTANT all additional amounts due upon receipt of invoice. CLIENT understands that any unpaid balances, after 30 days, shall incur interest accumulated at 1.5% monthly. **Retainer must be paid in full prior to scheduling or conducting any services.**

Rates – Hourly rates for Investigative Services, to include all travel time, report time, video and photo editing time, client consultation time, and case management time utilized on the investigation, shall be billed at $XX.XX per hour per investigator in fifteen-minute increments. Further expenses as determined necessary for the successful completion of the services to be provided by the INVESTIGATIVE CONSULTANT will be reimbursed 100%, and all mileage traveled will be billed at $0.XX per mile.

Credit Card Authorization / Chargeback or Payment Cancelation – CLIENT authorizes INVESTIGATIVE CONSULTANT to charge the CLIENT's credit card account, checking account, or other electronic payment account, provided to or used to pay, the INVESTIGATIVE CONSULTANT. The amounts charged by the INVESTIGATIVE CONSULTANT are for time, expenses, retainer, and billing as outlined in this agreement. CLIENT waives the right to chargeback or cancel any credit card, electronic payments (such as, but not limited to, PayPal, Venmo, etc.) or e-check, or written check payment.

CLIENT Interference / Misrepresentation – INVESTIGATIVE CONSULTANT reserves the right to terminate this agreement at any time if there is CLIENT interference or misrepresentation by CLIENT or second or third parties directed by CLIENT. Should this agreement be terminated due to CLIENT interference and or misrepresentation, the CLIENT will forfeit the entire retainer for the agreement.

Accuracy of Information – The accuracy of information submitted by the CLIENT will directly determine the success of the provided investigative services. INVESTIGATIVE CONSULTANT cannot be held liable for inaccuracies in public record information, databases accessed, or requests submitted by the CLIENT. While the information furnished by the

INVESTIGATIVE CONSULTANT is from reliable sources, its accuracy is not guaranteed. All information provided by the INVESTIGATIVE CONSULTANT should be verified as to accuracy, timeliness, and legal applications prior to preparation of reports or usage of information. Information provided may have items that are incomplete, incorrect, omitted, misspelled, or deleted. The accuracy of information provided is not in the control of the INVESTIGATIVE CONSULTANT. INVESTIGATIVE CONSULTANT shall attempt to maintain the integrity of all information and data provided. Information and data collected during this investigation shall be released to the CLIENT or other party intended as per the request of the CLIENT, at the sole discretion of the INVESTIGATIVE CONSULTANT.

No Warranties or Guarantee – Neither the INVESTIGATIVE CONSULTANT nor its employees or agents have made any warranties nor guarantees as to the success or outcome of the investigation, research, or matters involved in the investigative services to be provided for the CLIENT. CLIENT understands that investigations are, by their nature, limited by time and resources and may not produce the final product that the CLIENT had desired or intended.

Indemnification of INVESTIGATIVE CONSULTANT from CLIENT Provided Information – The CLIENT agrees to indemnify and hold the INVESTIGATIVE CONSULTANT, its employees, and agents harmless against all claims, damages, losses, expenses, liabilities and / or CLIENT or third-party actions arising out of or related to any information which the CLIENT provided to the INVESTIGATIVE CONSULTANT prior to or during the conduct of services provided. INVESTIGATIVE CONSULTANT, its employees, and agents shall not be liable for any legal, financial, incidental, or consequential damages of any type.

Refunds – Based on the nature of investigative work, we are unable to guarantee the desired result of the CLIENT. Therefore, we do not issue refunds for our services rendered. In the event there are unused retainer funds after all investigative services have been completed, the INVESTIGATIVE CONSULTANT shall refund all unused retainer funds within thirty days of completion of the investigation.

Termination of Agreement – This Agreement shall remain in effect until all retainer funds have been exhausted. or until all services are completed as agreed. This agreement may be terminated by either party with 48 hours written notification. If CLIENT terminates this agreement early for any reason, all scheduled work shall be billed at 50% (fifty percent). This agreement can be extended upon the acceptance and receipt of additional retainer funds at the discretion of the INVESTIGATIVE CONSULTANT.

Restraining / Protective Orders – Investigative Consultant will not conduct any investigative services or obtain any information for a CLIENT who has a restraining or protection order placed on them. In the event such an order is in place, and the CLIENT has not disclosed this information to the INVESTIGATIVE CONSULTANT, this agreement will be terminated upon discovery of this information by the INVESTIGATIVE CONSULTANT, and the full retainer shall be forfeit by the CLIENT.

Use of subcontractors – It is the discretion of the INVESTIGATIVE CONSULTANT to use subcontractors on an as-needed basis. INVESTIGATIVE CONSULTANT will only use qualified subcontractors with the proper licensing, insurance, and skills required. Due to assignment complexities, it may be necessary for the INVESTIGATIVE CONSULTANT to use multiple investigators throughout the assignment. Use of multiple investigators is at the discretion of the INVESTIGATIVE CONSULTANT.

Confidentiality – CLIENT understands that all provided findings, reports, videos, photos, data, and other investigative information from the INVESTIGATIVE CONSULTANT are exclusively for the use of the CLIENT. CLIENT agrees to limit access to these findings, reports, videos, photos, data, and other information to third parties who have a legitimate legal need to know and / or are authorized by law. CLIENT holds INVESTIGATIVE CONSULTANT, its employees, subcontractors, managers, owners, and other associates harmless from damages, losses, costs, and expenses, including attorney fees suffered or incurred due to claims based on investigative findings provided to the CLIENT. INVESTIGATIVE CONSULTANT will keep all investigative findings confidential and will not disseminate any findings to third parties unless authorized in writing by the CLIENT or ordered by a court of law in the United States of America.

Jurisdiction for Legal Proceedings – Any legal proceedings initiated by the CLIENT toward INVESTIGATIVE CONSULTANT shall be within Your County, Your State.

The validity of signatures on faxed, emailed, or other electronically disbursed versions of this contract shall be the same as the original.

_____   Date _____

CLIENT Signature

_____

CLIENT Name (Spelled)

_____   Date _____

INVESTIGATIVE CONSULTANT Signature

_____

INVESTIGATIVE CONSULTANT Name (Spelled)

About the Author

John L. Morris has been a professional private investigator since 2008. John desires to bring affordable yet sensible training opportunities to the private investigations industry utilizing his knowledge and experience from nearly 40 years in business and government management. His ambitious desires have led him to author multiple books, create over 100 training videos and conduct countless in-person and online training.

The author of the Book Series (How to be a Private Investigator) includes Business Basics for Private Investigators, Marketing Basics for Private Investigators, and Sales Basics for Private Investigators. He is also the founder of The PI Guy YouTube Channel, dedicated to free online training videos for the PI professional and those interested in learning more about the industry.

John carries PI licenses in multiple states to include Colorado and Wyoming. He has also been in leadership roles and a member of organizations such as PPIAC (Professional Private

Investigators Association of Colorado) , NCISS (National Council of Investigation & Security Services), ASIS International and Northern Colorado and Southern Wyoming Chapter, ACI (Association of Christian Investigators) , TALI (Texas Association of Licensed Investigators), CALI (California Association of Licensed Investigators), and FALI (Florida Association of Licensed Investigators). His experiences also include over 14 years of Local Government experience as Planning Commissioner, Chairman for the Planing Commission, City Councilman, Mayor Protem and Mayor for the city where he resides.